GEORGE FRIDERIC HANDEL

ZADOK THE PRIEST

Coronation Anthem for King George II, 1727

Text
I Kings i, 39-40

Edited by Donald Burrows

GW00721777

EDITOR'S NOTE

The opening choral entry of *Zadok the Priest*, with its seven-part spread of voices, is one of the most striking moments in the choral repertory. If possible, the full division of the voices throughout the work should be observed. This does not necessarily require a large choir, though of course it will work well with large numbers. Handel himself probably had about fifty singers for the first performance at the Coronation in 1727, and perhaps half that number when he included the anthem in his oratorios. Even if there are not sufficient altos and basses this anthem can still be performed quite effectively if all the altos take the Alto 1 line and the basses the Bass 2 line. It is not easy to reduce the soprano parts without more serious musical loss: if necessary some altos may be transferred to the Soprano 2 part.

This edition of *Zadok the Priest* is taken from the Novello Handel Edition of the *Four Coronation Anthems* edited by Donald Burrows and Damian Cranmer.

Order no. NOV290704

NOVELLO PUBLISHING LIMITED

8/9 Frith Street, LONDON, W1D 3JB
Tel +44 (0)20 7434 0066   Fax +44 (0)20 7287 6329

Orchestral material available from Music Sales Distribution Centre
Newmarket Road, Bury St Edmunds, Suffolk, IP33 3YB
Tel +44 (0)1284 702600   Fax +44 (0)1284 768301
Web: www.musicsales.com   e-mail: music@musicsales.co.uk

ISBN 0-7119-8862-5

9 780711 988620

ZADOK THE PRIEST

I Kings i, 39-40

GEORGE FRIDERIC HANDEL
edited by Donald Burrows

No. 1   Chorus ZADOK THE PRIEST

[Orchestral bass continues in quaver rhythm]

4

Chorus AND ALL THE PEOPLE REJOIC'D

6

No. 3   Chorus GOD SAVE THE KING

God save the King, long live the King. May the King live,

may the King live for e - ver, for e-ver, for e-ver, a-men,

* Last beat of b.39, Handel wrote f for Bass 2 and d for Bass 1: the latter was almost certainly an error.